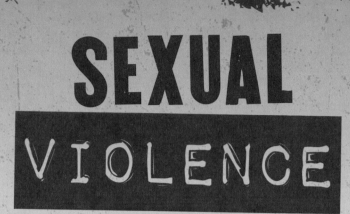

SEXUAL VIOLENCE

BY A.W. BUCKEY

INTOLERANCE
AND VIOLENCE
IN SOCIETY

ReferencePoint
Press®

San Diego, CA

For more information, contact:
ReferencePoint Press, Inc.
PO Box 27779
San Diego, CA 92198
www.ReferencePointPress.com

LIBRARY OF CONGRESS CATALOGING-IN-PUBLICATION DATA

Names: Buckey, A. W., author.
Title: Sexual violence / A.W. Buckey.
Description: San Diego, CA : ReferencePoint Press, [2020] | Series:
   Intolerance and violence in society | Includes bibliographical references
   and index.
Identifiers: LCCN 2019003265 (print) | LCCN 2019005082 (ebook) | ISBN
   9781682826942 (ebook) | ISBN 9781682826935 (hardcover)
Subjects: LCSH: Sex crimes--Juvenile literature. | Sexual abuse
   victims--Juvenile literature.
Classification: LCC HV6556 (ebook) | LCC HV6556 .B835 2020 (print) | DDC
   364.15/3--dc23
LC record available at https://lccn.loc.gov/2019003265

CONTENTS

IMPORTANT EVENTS IN THE HISTORY OF

INTOLERANCE AND VIOLENCE

1970s
The United States amends laws to stop requiring rape victims to provide evidence or eyewitness testimony in rape cases.

1980s
The term *date rape* is used to bring attention to sexual assaults committed by people who know their victims.

1890s
Early feminists, along with religious and working-class activists, convince state governments to raise the legal age of sexual consent in the United States.

1972
The first rape crisis center opens in the United States.

| 1890 | 1940 | 1970 | 1975 | 1980 |

1944
Activist Rosa Parks forms the Committee for Equal Justice for the Rights of Mrs. Recy Taylor, named for a black woman who was raped by six white men.

1975
The term *sexual harassment* is first used to describe demeaning sexual treatment of women in the workplace.

1977
A federal court rules that sexual harassment is a type of sex discrimination and is therefore illegal.

1994
The Rape, Abuse & Incest National Network (RAINN), the largest anti–sexual violence nonprofit, is founded.

2017
A news article revealing sexual violence committed by Hollywood producer Harvey Weinstein begins a second stage of the #MeToo movement.

2018
Dr. Denis Mukwege and Nadia Murad share the Nobel Peace Prize for their work against sexual violence in conflict situations.

1993
Marital rape becomes illegal in all 50 states.

2008
The UN Security Council declares that rape is a tool of war.

1990   2000   2005   2010   2020

2006
Tarana Burke starts the Me Too campaign to create solidarity among victims of sexual violence by helping them share their stories.

2018
Dr. Larry Nassar is sentenced to prison for his sexual assaults against the gymnasts and other athletes in his care.

1994
The US Congress passes the Violence Against Women Act (VAWA).

THE LARRY NASSAR
HEARING

In January 2018, Aly Raisman stood in front of a packed courtroom facing a row of TV cameras. A two-time Olympic gymnast and gold medalist, Raisman was not a stranger to crowds. But as she spoke, she told the courtroom that she had been nervous about that day. Raisman drew strength from the people who surrounded her and watched her. She was ready to speak out about her experience of sexual violence. Her testimony was part of the sentencing hearing of her abuser, Dr. Larry Nassar.

Nassar was a physician who worked with muscles and joints. He worked for the athletics department of Michigan State University. He was also an official doctor for USA Gymnastics, an organization that oversees the US national gymnastics teams. Nassar traveled to gymnastics meets and camps worldwide and met with hundreds of patients. He abused Raisman and hundreds of other athletes by pretending to perform medical procedures. Some of these patients were as young as six. Nassar fondled patients against their will. Often, he penetrated victims' vaginas with his fingers. This is what happened to Raisman. These actions were unwanted, and they caused lasting harm.

Raisman's words rang out in the courtroom as she spoke about the trauma and self-doubt that Nassar's actions had caused. "Abuse goes way beyond the moment, often haunting survivors for the rest

Olympic gymnast Aly Raisman reads her victim impact statement during a court hearing for Larry Nassar, a former gymnastics doctor. More than 100 gymnasts, including Raisman, testified that Nassar sexually abused them.

of their lives," she said.[1] She also pledged to find a way forward for herself and others. "I have both power and voice, and I am only beginning to just use them," Raisman said.[2]

NASSAR'S VICTIMS

Raisman was one of 156 girls and women who testified against Nassar. By October 2018, more than 400 people had accused Nassar of sexual abuse. Their accounts described many types of sexual violence. One woman testified that Nassar had raped her and filmed the rape. Others described abuse very similar to what Raisman experienced. Nassar also had child pornography. Possessing sexual images of children is a crime and a form of sexual violence.

Nassar had a pattern of targeting female athletes in his care, and most of his victims were girls and young women. But his abuse extended to male victims as well. Gymnast Jacob Moore was treated by Nassar in 2016. During a treatment that was supposedly for an injured shoulder, Nassar reportedly handled and discussed Moore's genitals. Moore was sixteen years old at the time of the abuse. At first, Moore did not want to talk publicly about what Nassar did to him. But eventually, he felt it was necessary to speak. "I don't want [other victims] to be scared to come out because of stigma that guys can't be sexually abused or taken advantage of," Moore said.[3]

"I don't want [other victims] to be scared to come out because of stigma that guys can't be sexually abused or taken advantage of." [3]

– *Jacob Moore, gymnast and survivor of sexual violence*

WAITING FOR JUSTICE

Accounts of Nassar's abuse stretch back to the 1990s. Nassar's behavior was well-known among the athletes he treated. His nickname was "the crotch doc."[4] Yet, somehow, he held onto powerful jobs for more than twenty years. John Manly, an attorney for Nassar's victims, described the case as "a perfect storm of sorts: of ineptitude, inaction, and neglect."[5]

Most of Nassar's victims were very young. Some told coaches and parents about Nassar's behavior and were not believed. Others were afraid to speak out, thinking that they must be wrong to feel violated by the doctor's actions. Rachel Denhollander was abused by

Nassar when she was a teenager. Later, she described her confusion and shame. "As Larry was abusing me each time, I thought it was fine because I thought I could trust the adults around me," Denhollander said.[6]

But many victims did file complaints against Nassar over the years. A 1998 lawsuit against a Michigan gym called Twistars contained complaints about his behavior. In 2014, a Michigan State student complained about abuse by Nassar. The university and police investigated, but no criminal charges were filed against the doctor. In 2015, USA Gymnastics stopped working with Nassar but did not warn other organizations about him. That same year, the Federal Bureau of Investigation (FBI) began investigating Nassar, but some of the victims who had filed complaints said the FBI never contacted them. Gina Nichols is the mother of one of Nassar's victims. Although her daughter gave information to the FBI, the agency never reached out. "I never got a phone call from the police or the FBI," Nichols remembers. "Not one person. Not one. Not one. Not one."[7]

THE AFTERMATH OF THE NASSAR CASE

At the January 2018 sentencing hearing, Nassar was sentenced to 40 to 175 years in prison. He had already pleaded guilty to possession of child pornography. Widespread media attention and public interest in the case forced the organizations that had employed Nassar to confront their role in the abuse. In January 2018, the entire board of USA Gymnastics was asked to resign. The board agreed to do so, and the organization hired new management.

As of May 2018, Michigan State University had agreed to pay $500 million to Nassar's victims. The university has also paid millions of dollars to defend a sexual violence case against former MSU dean

William Strampel, Nassar's boss. He is accused of sexually harassing female MSU students. Strampel is also criminally charged with willful neglect of duty for his role in the Nassar case. As of January 2019, his case was still pending. Strampel retired in July 2018 as MSU officials were trying to fire him.

SEXUAL VIOLENCE

Nassar's attacks on his patients were acts of sexual assault. *Sexual assault* is defined by the Rape, Abuse, and Incest National Network (RAINN) as "sexual contact or behavior that occurs without explicit consent of the victim."[8] This includes any sexual touching without consent. To give consent is to give permission. "Without explicit consent" means that, while the victim may not exactly say she does not want sexual contact to happen, she does not clearly show signs of wanting it to happen. Sometimes sexual assault occurs through physical force. But people who are verbally pressured or threatened into sexual activity also do not give explicit consent. Sexual assault is a common form of sexual violence.

Sexual violence is a term for many different acts, encompassing much more than what occurred in the Nassar case. Sexual violence is any unwanted or offensive sexual acts or sexual language. This includes rape, stalking, or verbal threats. The problem of sexual violence is widespread in society. While anyone can be a victim of sexual violence, women and girls are more likely to experience sexual violence in their lifetimes.

The Nassar case demonstrates many sobering facts about sexual violence in American society. Criminal penalties for sexual violence such as sexual assault and child pornography possession are severe. But victims of sexual violence often struggle to be heard and

10

USA Gymnastics and other organizations were criticized for the way they handled accusations against Nassar. Many of Nassar's victims had filed complaints about him in the years before he was convicted and sentenced to prison.

believed. Legal and social attitudes about sexual violence can add to the trauma these victims feel. Sexual violence is a pervasive and widely misunderstood issue. Today, victims' advocates and activists are working to expand and change society's understanding of sexual violence. By changing minds and breaking silences, they hope to prevent future violence.

WHAT IS THE HISTORY BEHIND
SEXUAL VIOLENCE?

Ancient stories about sexual violence portray sexual assaults as terrifying and harmful to victims. Folktales and myths have characters who suffer from assaults and attackers who are harshly punished. Nevertheless, throughout history, many forms of sexual violence have not been considered criminal or even morally wrong in society.

Ideas about sexual violence are deeply linked to ideas about sex and gender. For example, there is a long history of society seeing rape not as a form of violence but as a form of theft. Today, rape is a form of sexual assault, usually defined as forced penetration of a victim orally, vaginally, or anally. Attempted rape is another form of sexual assault. It happens when an attacker tries to rape someone. While terms like *sexual violence*, *sexual assault*, and *sexual harassment* were first used in the twentieth century, *rape* is an older word. In English, people first started to use the word *rape* to mean "forced sexual contact" in the 1400s.[9]

The ancient concept of rape as theft, not violence, was rooted in the historically traditional ideas that sex is supposed to be between a man and a woman and that women are the property of men. As an example of this concept, in the ancient Middle East, it was unlawful to rape some unmarried women. The Code of Hammurabi is an ancient set of laws from approximately 4,000 years ago. One of its rules stated that a man who raped a woman who was unmarried but belonged to another man should be put to death. However, these laws also allowed men to sell their daughters as wives to others and to force slaves into sexual relationships. The laws of the ancient Hebrew people punished some cases of rape. But they also held victims responsible for not trying to prevent the crime. For example, a woman who was raped outside the walls of a city was innocent, because her cries for help could not be heard. If she was raped inside a city, however, she was responsible for alerting others about the attack. If no one heard her cries, she was considered guilty of adultery, or sex

The mythical Greek god Zeus is depicted in ancient stories as a rapist. While it's unclear whether his rapes were condoned, he was worshipped by many people.

outside of marriage. The punishment for adultery was death for both people involved. The punishment for rape was paying money and getting married. According to the Torah's Book of Deuteronomy, a religious text, the rapist had to "pay [the victim's] father fifty shekels of silver. He must marry the young woman, for he has violated her."[10] In this way, victims of rape became the property of their attackers.

Old myths and stories often show these conflicting ideas about sexual violence. Ancient Greek myths, for example, were used to explain the religious beliefs of the culture. They have survived as inspiration for art and philosophy. Descriptions of sexual violence are common in these myths. Zeus, the head god of Greek mythology, is a repeat sexual assaulter. He rapes human women, often appearing in the form of an animal to do so. In one myth, Zeus also kidnaps a young man named Ganymede to be his lover. Zeus's sexual violence inspired fear in human beings and angered his wife, Hera. But it is not clear from these stories whether his violence was seen as wrong. Zeus's rapes did not keep him from being respected and worshipped as the king of the gods. Poseidon, the Greek god of the sea, was also a rapist. However, other Greek myths portray the act of rape as a horrifying violation. The Greek epic poem *The Iliad*, for example, describes the rape of a woman named Cassandra by a soldier named Ajax in the temple of the goddess Athena. The rape is portrayed as morally wrong.

SEXUAL VIOLENCE IN PREMODERN EUROPE

Many European cultures inherited and developed ancient ideas about sexual violence. In medieval England, it was a crime to rape an unmarried woman or girl. This crime was punishable by death in some cases. However, as in ancient rape laws, the victim was considered responsible for helping to prove the crime. She was expected to make a public accusation immediately after a rape. According to a thirteenth-century English legal writer, the victim was meant to "show [the public] the blood and her clothing stained with blood, and her torn garments."[11] In other words, only visibly violent attacks were considered punishable. In fact, it was common for women who accused others of rape to be arrested themselves. Almost half of medieval English women who claimed they were raped were arrested for allegedly making false accusations.

In medieval England, lawmakers decided on an age of consent for sexual activity. It became illegal for anyone to have sex with a person younger than age twelve, and later younger than ten, as children of those ages were considered incapable of giving consent. English law also developed the idea of coverture. This is a law that states that a

> **"[She must] show [the public] the blood and her clothing stained with blood, and her torn garments." 11**
>
> *— Requirement for rape victims in medieval England*

married man and woman become legally one person: the husband. Under laws of coverture, married women had no rights or identities outside of their husbands. This meant that a husband was allowed to rape his wife. A famous judge named Matthew Hale explained this concept in the 1600s: "The husband cannot be guilty of a rape committed by himself upon his lawful wife, for by their [marriage] the wife hath given up herself in this kind unto the husband which she cannot retract."[12]

SEXUAL VIOLENCE IN AMERICAN HISTORY

Sexual violence is part of the history of American conquest and war. During the American Revolutionary War (1775–1783), British soldiers raped colonial women and girls. When European Americans settled in California during the Gold Rush of the mid-1800s, they raped and killed Native Americans in large numbers.

Many American laws, including early rape laws, were inherited from the English legal system. Some American states set the age of consent between ten and twelve years old. There were laws against rape, but most had an exception for women who were considered impure, meaning women who were not virgins. If a rape victim had previous sexual experience, the rapist could claim that no crime occurred. This defense was often successful for accused rapists. In those cases, the accused rapists and victims were usually charged with lesser crimes instead. The American legal system also inherited the idea of coverture. Marital rape, which is rape within a marriage, was not considered a crime in the first centuries of American history.

It is difficult to know how many men and boys were victims of sexual violence in early American history. Homosexuality was legally banned in many parts of the United States. Sodomy laws prevented sex between two women or two men. These laws did not make distinctions between consensual and violent same-sex relationships. But there is evidence that sexual violence against men was sometimes punished. In 1625, a Virginia man named Richard Cornish was executed for sexually assaulting a male servant.

During the nineteenth century, women and people of color were banned from becoming lawyers, judges, or jury members, resulting in a legal system that heavily favored white men. This affected rape victims in court. "Until the middle of the twentieth century, rape victims in many states were required to provide corroboration in court, such as physical evidence or eyewitness testimony, because their word alone was not considered enough," journalist Bernice Yeung wrote.[13] Many of these laws lasted until the 1970s.

Black people who were enslaved in the United States in the nineteenth century had no legal protection from sexual violence. Sexual violence against slaves was legal, common, and widely accepted. Harriet Jacobs was born into slavery in the early 1800s. She escaped in 1842 and became an activist and writer. In her autobiography, Jacobs explained how enslaved girls and women were frequent targets of sexual violence. "The slave girl is reared in an atmosphere of [immoral sexuality] and fear," Jacobs wrote. "The lash and the foul talk of her master and his sons are her teachers. When she is fourteen or fifteen, her owner, or his sons, or the overseer, or perhaps all of them, begin to bribe her with presents. If these fail to

JEZEBELS AND BRUTES

During the slavery era, American society commonly portrayed black people with dehumanizing stereotypes. These stereotypes were promoted through images, fictional stories, and media reports. They wrongfully justified the violence that black slaves suffered. Two of these stereotypes, the Jezebel and the brute, were tied to ideas of sexual violence. The Jezebel stereotype was a highly sexual black woman. She was often portrayed in images as naked or wearing little clothing. Jezebels were shown as crude, immoral women who constantly desired sex. According to this false stereotype, black women were not really victimized by white men; instead, they desired and sought out sex with white men. In this way, the Jezebel stereotype distorted the true nature of sexual violence against black women.

The brute was the male counterpart to this stereotype. Brutes were portrayed as large, muscular black men with scary sexual desires. Stories about brutes stoked fears that they sought to capture and rape white women. In many cases, the false stereotype of dangerous brutes was used to justify violence against black men, including public lynchings. In reality, most white victims of sexual violence were attacked by white men. The brute, like the Jezebel, was a myth used to justify and promote violence against black people. Although it is no longer as widely acceptable to portray black people in these stereotypical ways, some depictions of the brute and the Jezebel have survived into the present day.

accomplish their purpose, she is whipped or starved into submission to their will."[14] Female slave owners also sexually assaulted their male slaves. Sexual violence against servants who were not enslaved was also common.

Activists began to speak out against sexual violence. In the 1800s, abolitionists, or anti-slavery activists, protested the widespread sexual violence against slaves. In the late 1800s, several groups fought to end sexual violence against young girls. This included religious groups, laborers, and suffragists, early feminists who began lobbying for women's right to vote in the late 1800s. After encouragement from activists, by 1900 most states had raised the legal age of sexual consent from ten to between fourteen and eighteen. Early feminists also called for women to start serving on juries. These changes helped pave the way for a broader understanding of sexual violence. They introduced the idea that it was violent for men to have sexual contact with young girls, slaves, or servants.

ACTIVISM AGAINST SEXUAL VIOLENCE

The civil rights movement battled for the legal rights of African Americans in the United States. After the American Civil War (1861–1865) ended, many Southern states instituted policies of racial segregation. Under racial segregation, black people were barred from some public spaces, officially denied certain jobs and roles, and forced to attend separate, or segregated, schools. Racial discrimination was widespread throughout the country. The civil rights movement of the 1950s and 1960s sought to end segregation and racial discrimination. The movement's work included efforts to end the terror of sexual violence against black women during this time.

Rosa Parks is one of the most famous activists of the civil rights movement. She is remembered by history for a brave act of civil disobedience—refusing to move to the back of a bus in Montgomery, Alabama, in 1955. This act help spark the Montgomery Bus Boycott, a protest against the segregated bus system. But before she helped begin the boycott, Parks worked on cases of sexual violence. Parks joined the National Association for the Advancement of Colored People (NAACP) in 1943. Parks had been sexually assaulted by a white neighbor in 1931. She knew from experience that sexual violence was part of the widespread racial injustice that black people experienced under segregation, and she fought to end this violence.

In 1944, a black Alabama woman named Recy Taylor was abducted and raped by six white men. Taylor, who was twenty-four, reported the rape to police. Her report resulted in a $250 fine against the man who owned the car used to abduct Taylor. When Parks heard about the case, she formed the Committee for Equal Justice for the Rights of Mrs. Recy Taylor. The committee spread to forty-one states, working to raise awareness of the case. Five years later, after a black woman named Gertrude Perkins was raped by two white police officers, Parks started a similar committee. However, Taylor's and Perkins's attackers were never convicted in relation to the assaults. "They didn't try to do nothing about it," Taylor remembers.[15] In fact, during the segregation era, not one Southern white man was convicted of sexual assault against a black woman.

In the 1960s and 1970s, the Second Wave of the feminist movement advocated for more professional, social, and political power for women. Ending sexual violence against women in the workplace and in personal relationships became a priority of the movement. In the 1970s, feminists began holding marches called Take Back the Night. These marches drew attention to the threats of violence that women faced in public places. Today, the Take Back the Night Foundation still sponsors events and protests against sexual violence.

In the 1970s, journalist Susan Brownmiller became active in feminism, joining a group called the New York Radical Feminists. This group and others like it gave women a chance to share common experiences. Brownmiller was surprised by the number of women who shared stories of sexual violence. She decided to research the history of rape. Her research resulted in a book called *Against*

The civil rights movement sought to end segregation and racial discrimination in all areas of society. This included some activists' work toward raising awareness about the widespread problem of sexual violence against black women.

Our Will: Men, Women, and Rape, published in 1975. In the book, Brownmiller writes, "Rape is a . . . conscious process of intimidation by which *all* men keep *all* women in a state of fear."[16] Brownmiller's analysis was shocking and influential. It was criticized by other feminist scholars, such as Angela Davis. Davis, who is black, said the book was "pervaded with racist ideas."[17] She said Brownmiller's writing supported stereotypes of black men as sexually violent. But the book also became an emblem of new way of thinking about sexual violence. It helped introduce the idea that sexual violence was a widespread social problem. It also helped popularize the idea that sexual violence and gender discrimination are deeply related.

NEW CONCEPTS OF SEXUAL VIOLENCE

In the second half of the twentieth century, activists started using new terms to describe underdiscussed forms of sexual violence. In 1975, a group of women used the words *sexual harassment* to describe how they were being treated at work. The following year, the women's magazine *Redbook* surveyed readers about their experiences with sexual harassment. Eighty percent of respondents said that they had been sexually harassed at work. The 1964 Civil Rights Act outlawed sex discrimination at work. In 1977, a federal court decided that sexual harassment should be understood as a type of sex discrimination.

Organizations and lawmakers began to address sexual violence. The first rape crisis centers opened in 1972. These centers offer resources to victims of sexual violence such as counseling and help with legal matters. The same year, the US Congress passed Title IX, part of a larger law called the Education Amendments of 1972. Title IX prevents sex discrimination in schools that receive federal funding. Title IX helped put systems in place for addressing sexual violence in schools and universities. For example, Title IX requires schools to have an established way of dealing with sexual discrimination complaints and allegations of sexual violence.

The term *date rape* was first used in the 1980s. Psychologist Mary Koss was one of the first researchers to use the term to describe sexual violence between acquaintances, friends, or romantic partners. Koss's research found that more than 7 percent of male college students had forced or tried to force someone into sex. Almost none of the men who admitted to this behavior thought they had committed a crime. Many people still believed rape could only occur when the attacker was a stranger who used weapons or extreme physical force. Talking about date rape became a way to draw attention to the more common occurrence of rape between acquaintances. Today, however, antiviolence activists prefer not to use the term *date rape*. They worry that the word *date* can make this type of rape seem less common or less serious than it really is. The terms *sexual assault* or *rape* are preferred.

Although society was starting to recognize the problems of sexual harassment and rape between acquaintances, it was still legal in many states for a husband to sexually assault his wife. In 1984, the New York case of Mario and Denise Liberta drew attention to the crime of marital rape. Mario Liberta was an abusive husband, and his wife, Denise, had gotten several restraining orders against him. In 1981, however, Liberta took his wife to a motel and raped her in front of their two-year-old son. Liberta did not deny the crime. "I don't think it was anybody's business," he said of the criminal charges.[18] Three years later, Liberta became the first New Yorker convicted of marital rape. By 1993, marital rape was illegal in every US state.

> **"I don't think it was anybody's business."** [18]
> —*Mario Liberta, on his rape of his wife in 1981*

In 1994, Congress passed the Violence Against Women Act (VAWA). This act has provided federal funding for rape crisis centers and other efforts to prevent sexual assault. It has also helped provide information and resources to people dealing with the aftermath of sexual violence. VAWA was updated and reauthorized in 2000, 2005, and 2013. Despite proposals to reauthorize VAWA again in 2018, the act expired that December because Congress failed to pass budget measures that included VAWA funding. The proposals to reauthorize VAWA remained unresolved in February 2019.

HOW DOES SEXUAL
VIOLENCE HAPPEN?

In the United States, one in six women and one in thirty-three men are victims of rape or attempted rape in their lifetimes. These statistics do not include the larger number of people who experience sexual assault and sexual harassment. Although anyone can commit or suffer from sexual violence, most sexual violence victims are female and most attackers are male. Women from ages eighteen to twenty-four are the most common adult victims of sexual assault. Children from ages twelve to seventeen are the most common child victims of sexual assault. Crimes of sexual violence are frequently committed and often not punished. For example, it's estimated that for every 1,000 rapes, an average of 4.6 perpetrators are arrested, charged with a crime, convicted, and sent to prison. This rate is lower than the punishment rate for several nonsexual crimes such as robbery and assault. Furthermore, many acts of sexual violence are never reported, largely due to sensitivity and stigmas around the issue. However, research has still revealed patterns in the types of people who commit sexual violence.

WHO COMMITS SEXUAL VIOLENCE?

Any person can commit sexual violence. There is no one typical rapist, assailant, or sexual harasser. However, there are patterns in the types of people who commit sexual violence, especially those who

Women are the victims of sexual violence far more often than men. However, anyone can become a victim of sexual violence.

attack more than once. Most people who commit sexual violence are male. However, researchers point out that among men who are coerced or threatened into unwanted sex, most are victimized by women. About half of perpetrators of sexual violence are more than thirty years old. Another quarter are in their twenties. People who commit crimes of sexual violence are likely to commit other crimes as well. Attackers usually commit sexual violence against people they know. Most sexual assaults involve one perpetrator and one victim. However, approximately 6 percent of sexual assaults involve multiple perpetrators.

Research suggests that many rapes and sexual assaults are committed by repeat offenders. In other words, sexually violent

DRUGS AND SEXUAL ASSAULT

There are certain drugs that people may use in committing sexual assault. These drugs, commonly known as date rape drugs, help attackers put their victims in a vulnerable state. Some common date rape drugs are GHB, ketamine, and rohypnol (known as roofies). They can be put into victims' drinks without their knowledge. GHB and rohypnol cause sleepiness and forgetfulness. These drugs can make victims pass out and forget what happens to them during their sleep. Ketamine can cause users to lose control of their movements and sense of time. Other similar drugs include Ambien, scopolamine, and benzodiazepines. In large doses, drugs like GHB can cause death.

Although the term date rape drug is well known, experts generally do not use that term. They prefer to call these attacks drug-facilitated sexual assaults. Many prescription and illegal drugs are used in sexual assaults, but the most common sexual assault drug is alcohol. Alcohol consumption can cause victims to lose control of their movements, fall asleep, or lose their memories. Perpetrators of sexual violence often encourage their victims to become drunk. They may also target victims who have already been drinking.

people tend to have multiple victims. These repeat offenders tend to initially cross sexual boundaries in early adulthood and continue to be sexually violent as they grow older.

In the early 2000s, psychologists David Lisak and Paul M. Miller decided to research what they called "undetected rapists."[19] These were people who had committed sexual violence but had not been arrested or charged with crimes. Lisak and Miller wanted to understand how these undetected rapists viewed their own actions. The two researchers designed a confidential survey that asked people about their experiences committing sexual violence. But they described acts of sexual violence without using words like *rape*. Lisak and Miller found that many undetected rapists showed high levels of narcissism and entitlement. They felt they could act as they wished and did not think about the effects their actions would have on others. "They lack the ability to see what they do from the perspective of their victims," Lisak explained.[20] The researchers found that many of the people they surveyed didn't think of themselves as sexually violent. Even after admitting to acts that fit the definition of rape, they did not identify as criminals. These attackers believed common stereotypes about sexual violence. Because they did not attack total strangers or use weapons, they did not think of themselves as committing repeated acts of rape.

THE EFFECTS OF SEXUAL VIOLENCE

Sexual violence affects victims physically, mentally, and emotionally. These effects can be severe. Victims often continue hurting for many years after an instance of sexual violence occurs; the effects can last throughout a victim's lifetime. Victims of physically violent attacks can suffer injuries such as bruising, cuts, and internal bleeding. Rape victims are in danger of contracting sexually transmitted infections (STIs) or of becoming pregnant. Being a victim of sexual assault increases a person's risk of suicide by a factor of ten.

Victims of sexual violence are also at risk of eating disorders, self-harm, and substance abuse. All of these behaviors can be ways of coping with trauma and stress. When the writer Roxane Gay was twelve years old, she was raped by a group of boys she knew. After the attack, she began eating compulsively. "I was broken, and to numb the pain of that brokenness, I ate and ate and ate," Gay writes.[21] Gaining weight gave her a sense of protection. "I was trapped in my body. . . . I was miserable, but I was safe. Or at least I could tell myself I was safe," she writes.[22]

A 2018 study found that middle-aged women who had experienced sexual assault were more likely to suffer from anxiety, depression, and sleep problems. Women who had been sexually harassed at work were more likely to have sleep problems and high blood pressure. The head author of the study, psychologist Rebecca Thurston, emphasized that these effects last for a long time after the violence. "These are experiences that [a woman] could have had long ago . . . and it can have this long arm of influence throughout a woman's life," Thurston said.[23]

Sometimes, victims of sexual violence develop post-traumatic stress disorder (PTSD). PTSD is a psychiatric disorder that affects people who have been through traumatic experiences. People with PTSD often experience flashbacks to the traumatic event. They may be troubled by these memories, which are intense and disturbing. PTSD can cause people to feel detached from everyday life. People who suffer from PTSD may feel sensitive to certain sights, sounds, and behaviors.

CHRISTINE BLASEY FORD AND REMEMBERING SEXUAL VIOLENCE

In the summer of 2018, a US Supreme Court confirmation battle put the national spotlight on the issue of sexual violence and memory. Christine Blasey Ford is a research psychologist and professor. In July 2018, Ford called her congressional representative's office and left a message about Brett Kavanaugh, a federal appeals court judge. When Ford made this phone call, Kavanaugh was on President Donald Trump's short-list of potential nominees to serve

Christine Blasey Ford speaks at Supreme Court justice Brett Kavanaugh's confirmation hearing, describing her memories of him sexually assaulting her. Kavanaugh was eventually confirmed to the Supreme Court.

on the Supreme Court. Ford alleged that Kavanaugh had tried to rape her when they were both in high school. They had been at a party together, Ford remembered, and Kavanaugh had been drinking heavily. Ford said that Kavanaugh and his friend had held her down on a bed. Kavanaugh, she remembered, had tried to take her clothes off and had covered her mouth when she tried to scream.

Trump eventually nominated Kavanaugh. All Supreme Court nominees must go through a hearing in front of members of the US Senate before they are confirmed to the position of Supreme Court justice. The purpose of the hearing is to decide if the nominee is fit to serve on the Supreme Court. Once Kavanaugh was nominated, Ford sent a letter detailing her story about him to Democratic Senator Dianne Feinstein, who was on the Senate committee that reviews Supreme Court nominees. Based on Ford's experience, she and her supporters felt Kavanaugh was unfit to be a Supreme Court justice.

"Indelible in the hippocampus is the laughter." [24]

– Christine Blasey Ford, describing lasting memories of a sexual assault

Ford agreed to publicly testify at Kavanaugh's confirmation hearing. She was asked what she remembered most about the judge's sexual assault against her. "Indelible in the hippocampus is the laughter," Ford replied.[24] Kavanaugh and his friend had laughed, she said, as they attempted to rape her. When Ford said that this part of the memory was "indelible in the hippocampus," she was talking about the way the brain processes traumatic events. The hippocampus is the part of the brain that stores long-term memories. When people go through a traumatic event like attempted rape, their memories are both fragmented and extremely strong. Some parts of the event may be fuzzy, or blocked out. Other details may leave an unusually sharp and strong memory behind. The laughter Ford heard is one of those unforgettable sensory details. She was saying that the memory has stayed with her, unchanged, for her entire life since the event. However, Kavanaugh denied Ford's claims in his own emotional testimony. He was eventually confirmed by the US Senate and sworn in as a Supreme Court judge.

DOMESTIC VIOLENCE AND REPRODUCTIVE CONTROL

Domestic violence, also called intimate partner violence, is the practice of abusing a partner in a romantic relationship. Intimate partner violence can involve physical violence such as slapping or punching, as well as verbal threats. Sometimes it is sexual violence. Abusers may use demeaning sexual language or unwanted sexual touching to control and intimidate their partners. They may mock their partners' sexual behavior. Domestic abusers may also rape or threaten to rape their partners.

Reproductive control is another form of domestic sexual violence. It occurs when someone uses peer pressure or tricks to influence decisions about pregnancy. This might involve trying to make a partner pregnant against her will. For example, an abuser might hide a partner's birth control or remove a condom without permission. An abuser might also try to force a partner to have or not have an abortion. These tactics are forms of sexual violence. They take away a person's right to make informed decisions about sex and pregnancy.

Lying about sexually transmitted infections is another way of taking away a person's right to informed sexual consent. People who do not disclose that they have an STI take away their partner's right to accurately weigh the risks of sexual contact.

SEXUAL VIOLENCE IN SCHOOLS

Sexual violence often occurs in communities and organizations such as schools or workplaces. In K–12 schools, both students and staff members have been known to commit sexual violence. A 2017 investigation found that between 2011 and 2015, there were 17,000 reports of sexual violence by students in K–12 schools in the United States. Experts believe that the actual number of incidents is much

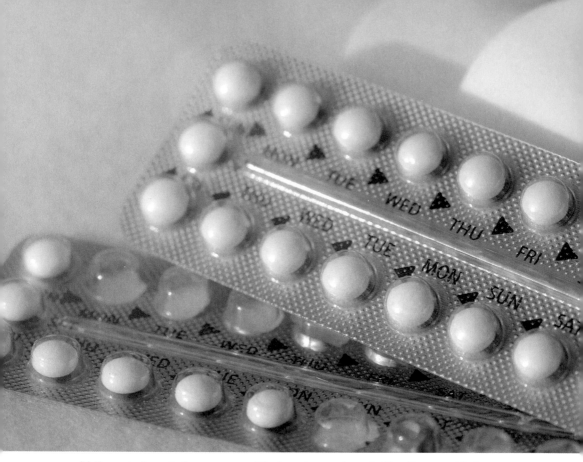

Birth control can help women and their partners plan whether they want to become pregnant. But an abuser may hide his partner's birth control pills or find other ways to take away her power over decisions about pregnancy.

higher. Researchers found that the number of incidents increased when students started middle school.

Sexual violence is also common on college campuses. According to the documentary film *The Hunting Ground*, the rates of sexual assaults at colleges and universities have been described as an "epidemic."[25] About 11 percent of students are sexually assaulted during college. One reason for this could be that many sexual predators begin attacking in their late teens or early twenties. In addition, rates of sexual assault among eighteen- to twenty-four-year-old women who do not attend college are higher than those for college students.

SEXUAL VIOLENCE IN WORKPLACES

According to Stop Street Harassment, 81 percent of women and 43 percent of men have experienced sexual harassment. Much of this harassment happened in public places. For example, street harassment, also known as cat calling, is when harassers (usually men) make unsolicited comments to people (usually women) who pass by them on the street or in other places. However, 38 percent of women and 13 percent of men reported being sexually harassed at work.

Some work harassment happens between coworkers at different professional levels, as there are differences in power between people with different jobs. A worker at a factory, for example, cannot give explicit consent to her supervisor if she is worried that he will fire her for turning down sex. A security guard cannot avoid his boss's sexual comments if he is unable to leave his desk during his shift. Workplace sexual abusers use these power differences to trap and scare their victims. Often, workers who are targeted for sexual harassment do not get meaningful support from their management. A 2017 survey of 400 company directors found that the majority of company boards did not discuss issues of workplace sexual harassment.

In September 2018, McDonald's workers in ten US cities went on strike to protest sexual harassment at their workplaces and the company's response to the problem. Workers shared stories of physical assaults, verbal sexual harassment, and threats. They also shared the ways in which the company had failed to address the issue. When Breauna Matthews was fifteen and working as a McDonald's cashier, an older employee made comments about her body and asked her for sex. When she reported the behavior to a manager, she said he reportedly told her "you will never win that

Any unwanted touch or sexual comment is sexual harassment. This behavior happens in workplaces, schools, and elsewhere.

battle."[26] Other employees reported that they feared losing their jobs for reporting sexual harassment. The strikers pointed out that in 2018, ten female McDonald's employees had filed sexual harassment complaints with the US government.

McDonald's employees are not alone in their experiences of widespread harassment. According to a 2016 survey, 40 percent of female fast food employees are sexually harassed at work. As Adriana Alvarez, an activist and McDonald's employee, said to the *Guardian* newspaper, "[Sexual harassment] happens to everybody. It cuts across all classes."[27]

Sexual harassment is also widespread in the US military. Approximately 1.29 million people are active members of the military. About 16 percent of these active duty members are women. From

September 2016 to September 2017, a total of 6,769 active duty members reported being victims of sexual violence. Most of these reports were from women. Experts estimate that these numbers represent about one-third of the incidents that actually happened. Many military women say that it can be difficult to speak out about sexual violence in their organizations. This is especially true if their attacker is someone within their chain of command and therefore has professional power over them. Victims of sexual violence say they've experienced retaliation from other service members after speaking out. "There is a lot of victim-shaming that happens," says Kim Speedy, a military counselor.[28]

SEXUAL VIOLENCE AGAINST CHILDREN

Children of all ages can be victims of sexual violence. Sexual violence against children can include unwanted touching and groping, verbal sexual harassment, and rape. Sexual violence against children is sometimes called molestation. People who sexually pursue children are sometimes called pedophiles. Children are too young to consent to sexual activity. All sexual contact between adults and children is sexual violence.

It is estimated that one in four girls and one in six boys experience sexual violence during childhood. The vast majority of the time, the abuser is a person the child knows. In many cases, the child's attacker is a relative, trusted friend, or authority figure such as a priest or coach. Children also commit acts of sexual violence against each other.

Child sexual violence has lasting traumatic effects. Child victims of sexual violence often struggle not to blame themselves for the abuse they experience. They may feel guilty that they were unable to stop

PORNOGRAPHY AND SEXUAL VIOLENCE

Pornography, or porn, is sexual imagery that is designed to sexually arouse the people who view it. Much of pornography portrays consensual sexual activity. But some pornography depicts or records acts of sexual violence. All child pornography is considered sexual violence because it portrays child molestation. For this reason, child pornography is illegal, even when the acts depicted are fake.

Some people argue that all pornography encourages sexual violence. They believe that the types of sexual acts shown in pornography are violent and demeaning to women. Feminist scholar Catharine MacKinnon, for example, says, "[Pornography promotes] a range of atrocities and violence to women in ways that often the people who are committing those acts don't experience as being violent." Others, including researchers of human sexuality, do not see a direct link between pornography and sexual violence.

Quoted in Kate Halford, "The Pornography Phenomenon - Catharine MacKinnon," YouTube, December 7, 2016. www.youtube.com.

or speak out against their attackers. Adult survivors of child sexual abuse may have trouble trusting others or having romantic and sexual relationships. In addition, people who experience sexual violence as children are more likely to be targeted for sexual violence as adults.

It can be very difficult for child victims of sexual violence to get help and find justice. Children who are victimized may not understand what has happened to them. Children's understandings of sexuality and violence grow and change over time. They may lack the vocabulary to describe the abuse they've suffered. In addition, the vast power difference between adult abusers and child victims makes it easier for attackers to silence their victims. Sexual abusers may use lying, manipulation, and threats to keep their victims from speaking out. Brad, who chose to share only his first name, was sexually abused as a child by a sports trainer. This trainer lied to Brad, telling him that the abuse was a way to help him succeed athletically. As a young boy, Brad trusted the trainer's words. He believed that the shame and guilt he felt about the abuse were his fault.

Like adult victims of sexual violence, child victims often struggle to be heard and believed. Victims who do speak out may be faced with inaction, or they may find that their friends and relatives choose to side with their abusers. Navila Rashid, a social worker, was sexually assaulted by family friends and a relative in her childhood. Although the abuse left her feeling ashamed, disgusted, and afraid, she says, "I didn't recognize it was sexual until I was much older."[29] Later, Rashid decided to tell her mother about the abuse. "She told me, well, at least you weren't raped," Rashid recalls. "[She said] maybe it's a good thing that it happened to you, because it makes you stronger."[30] Even as a child, Rashid knew that her mother was wrong to react that way. Still, she could not ignore the hurt her mother's reaction caused her. She felt unsupported and misunderstood.

The silence, shame, and denial surrounding child sexual violence helps abusers commit multiple crimes without punishment. Larry Nassar is one example of a predator who was able to attack multiple victims, in part because victims were afraid to speak or not believed when they did speak up. Another example comes from the Catholic Church. In many parts of the world, Catholic priests have used their power to abuse children. In August 2018, a grand jury in Pennsylvania released a report on sexual abuse in the Catholic Church there. It found that more than 300 priests had abused more than 1,000 children over a period of seventy years. Most of the children abused were boys. The report pointed out that leaders of the Catholic Church had helped ignore or cover up many of these incidents of abuse, which allowed the priests to attack again and again. The report helped document hundreds of these cases, and the way that the larger organization had protected offenders. The grand jury reported that "the failure to prevent abuse was a systemic failure, an institutional failure."[31] As a result of the report, US Department of Justice prosecutors began investigating seven Catholic dioceses, or religious districts, in Pennsylvania. Prosecutors in Illinois, Missouri, New Jersey, and New Mexico began investigating dioceses in their own states.

"The failure to prevent abuse was a systemic failure, an institutional failure." [31]

– report of a Pennsylvania grand jury on sexual abuse in the Pennsylvania Roman Catholic Church

Statutory rape is another form of sexual violence that affects children. In early American history, girls as young as ten were considered old enough to consent to sex with adults. Today, the US legal age of sexual consent varies by state. It ranges from sixteen to eighteen. Sexual activity involving people younger than the age of consent is known as statutory rape. Statutory rape laws are complex. In some US states, there is one legal age of consent, such as eighteen. According to the law, no one younger than that age can consent to sexual activity. Other statutory rape laws are designed to prevent sexual activity between people with large age differences. Under these laws, a person over the age of consent cannot have sexual activity with someone who is under a certain age.

SEXUAL VIOLENCE AGAINST THE LGBT COMMUNITY

Because sexual violence damages its victims' health and safety, it is an effective tool of oppression and discrimination. Sexual violence can be a way to maintain control over those with less power in society. In addition, people with less social, legal, and economic power are more vulnerable to sexual attacks. For example, living in poverty increases a person's risk of experiencing sexual violence. Members of the LGBT (lesbian, gay, bisexual, and transgender) community, especially women and girls, are at increased risk of sexual violence, including violence that specifically targets them because of their gender identity or sexual orientation.

Sexual violence has been used as a tool to punish members of the LGBT community. This phenomenon is called homophobic rape. Attackers target gay, lesbian, or transgender victims to force them into heterosexual sex. This crime is well documented in South Africa, where it became known as *corrective rape*. This term came from attackers' false claims that they could correct homosexuality through sexual violence. Homophobic rape also occurs in other parts of the world. Lesbian women are at especially high risk of homophobic rape.

Sexual violence is used against LGBT people in many other ways as well. According to the Human Rights Campaign, an organization that advocates for the LGBT community, bisexual women are at an especially high risk of sexual violence. Transgender people also suffer from high rates of sexual violence. A 2015 survey found that almost half of all transgender people are sexually assaulted during their lifetimes. LGBT advocates point out that discrimination can make LGBT people more vulnerable to violence. For example, teens who come out as gay or transgender are sometimes disowned by their families. These teens are more likely to become homeless and are

Members of the LGBT community have historically been at high risk for sexual violence. However, there are several organizations that are working to stop discrimination and violence against LGBT people.

therefore more vulnerable to sexual attacks. Sarah McBride, who works for the Human Rights Campaign, is a transgender woman and a survivor of sexual violence. She spoke about the way that anti-transgender stereotypes affect discussions of sexual violence: "There's this extra unique barrier that transgender [sexual assault survivors] face around this notion that . . . we are somehow so undesirable that people wouldn't sexually assault us."[32] In this sense, transgender victims of sexual violence may face extra obstacles to get authorities and others to believe their stories. McBride hopes that speaking about her experiences can help dissolve those harmful stereotypes.

SEXUAL VIOLENCE AGAINST NATIVE AMERICANS

In the United States, Native Americans have experienced many centuries of oppression. Today, Native American women experience higher rates of sexual violence than any other American racial group. In 2010, the Urban Indian Health Institute and the Centers for Disease Control and Prevention (CDC) surveyed 148 Native American women living in Seattle, Washington. Ninety-four percent of the surveyed women had experienced sexual violence. About half of all Native American women experience sexual violence during their lifetimes. Most of them are attacked by white men. In the United States, Native American reservations have their own tribal courts. Until a change in federal law in 2013, these tribal courts were not able to prosecute non–Native Americans for sexual assault. This meant that it was easy for non–Native Americans to attack people on Native American land and escape consequences. Because of the tribal courts' limited power, if a non–Native American committed a sexual violence crime against a Native American on tribal land, the case had to be referred to federal US attorneys for prosecution. Between 2005 and 2009, US attorneys only prosecuted one-third of the sexual violence cases that Native American governments referred to them.

Sexual violence affects every part of modern society. It takes many forms and is present in all major institutions, as well as in private life. Patterns of victimization show that people with less power are often more vulnerable to sexual violence, and that sexual violence can be a tool to maintain power over others. Society's response to sexual violence reflects this. Powerful institutions and powerful people often fail to effectively respond to sexual violence, and people with less power find it difficult to get justice.

HOW DOES SOCIETY RESPOND TO

SEXUAL VIOLENCE?

Today, acts of sexual violence such as rape and sexual assault are considered very serious crimes. In the United States, a sexual assault conviction can result in a prison sentence of up to twenty years. Sexual violence is widely condemned. Rapists and child sexual abusers are unacceptable in society.

However, toxic ideas persist about the nature of sexual violence. Sometimes, these beliefs and ideas show up in subtle ways, such as assumptions that people may not even be aware they have or common media narratives. These beliefs include the ideas that sexual violence must be physically destructive to be real; that victims must go to great lengths to prove that sexual violence occurred; and that only young, pure, unmarried women can be victims of sexual crimes. Responses to sexual violence in the legal system, in organizations, and in culture all reflect these beliefs. These responses often dismiss the harm done to the victim, seek to excuse the attacker, or deny the attack happened altogether.

POLICE AND LEGAL RESPONSES

Many people assume that the best response to sexual violence is a complaint to the police. Police officers are tasked with investigating

A group of people protest against sexual violence. Advocates against sexual violence argue that the issue affects all people, not just those who are directly harmed by sexual abuse.

incidents of sexual violence. Officers must talk to victims and get their stories. They investigate by interviewing suspects and finding witnesses and evidence. However, about 84 percent of sexual assaults are never reported to the police. Many cases of sexual violence reported to the police are never investigated; even fewer cases result in an arrest. There are a few key reasons why this is the case.

One reason police do not investigate crimes of sexual violence is that they often do not believe victims who come forward. From 2004 to 2006, sociologist Martin Schwartz researched police officers' attitudes toward rape reports. Schwartz found that more than a quarter of police officers believed that most rape reports were false.

When police officers do not believe sexual assault victims' stories, it can make it nearly impossible for victims to get justice. Without proper police investigation, perpetrators of sexual assault are not arrested.

In other words, these officers believed that the majority of people who told police they had been raped were lying. Research shows that most people do not lie about being the victim of any crime, including rape. Experts believe that fewer than one percent of rape reports are false. But the average officer disbelieved approximately one-third of rape reports, according to Schwartz's study. This disbelief affects every stage of the investigation process for sexual assault cases.

Police officers who are skeptical of victims are more likely to dismiss reports and less likely to collect evidence. Essentially, these officers are more likely to just not investigate sexual assault reports. Research on police practices found that many departments release misleading information about sexual violence. A study of police department practices in Baltimore, Maryland; New Orleans, Louisiana; Philadelphia, Pennsylvania; and Saint Louis, Missouri, showed that the departments undercounted incidents of rape in three ways: "designating a complaint as 'unfounded' with little or no investigation; classifying an incident as a lesser offense; and, failing to create a written report that a victim made a rape complaint."[33] In other words, many reported rapes were never acknowledged or recorded by police in these cities. Further research showed similar practices in about a quarter of large American police departments.

Victims who do approach the police after sexual violence often report being treated in dismissive or inappropriate ways. In the 2015 book *Missoula*, Jon Krakauer examined how police in Missoula, Montana, responded to multiple sexual assaults against young women. One of the women, Kerry Barrett, recalled her experience of reporting an attempted rape to the police. She remembers a police officer asking her if she had a boyfriend. When she told him she did not, she asked why he was asking. "And he said something to the effect of 'Well, sometimes girls cheat on their boyfriends, and regret it, and then claim they were raped,'" Barrett recalls.[34] Barrett was taken aback by the officer's attitude. Eventually, the police decided not to press charges against Barrett's alleged attacker.

In addition, victims of sexual violence who do not trust the police are less likely to report sexual crimes. Black women are at increased risk of violence at the hands of police. They are also less likely than white women to report acts of sexual violence to the police. Immigrants to the United States are less likely to report crimes than native-born US citizens are. Many immigrants report that they do not approach the police about crimes because they are scared of discrimination or threats of deportation. This fear of contacting authorities can make immigrants especially vulnerable to sexual violence.

Police officers can be perpetrators of sexual violence as well. Their ability to arrest and use physical force gives them a lot of power over other people. Daniel Holtzclaw was a police officer in Oklahoma City, Oklahoma. He used his power as a police officer to commit sexual assault and rape. Holtzclaw targeted black women from low-income neighborhoods. He sexually assaulted women after stopping them, as a police officer, to question them. For example, Holtzclaw attacked one victim after stopping her car late at night. He asked her to prove she was sober, then sexually assaulted her. In 2015, Holtzclaw was convicted of eighteen crimes and sentenced to 263 years in prison. Although Holtzclaw's case resulted in a conviction, experts believe that incidences of sexual violence by police officers are underreported. Between 2005 and 2013, approximately 400 police officers were arrested for sexual violence. But a report on police sexual violence estimated that the actual number of incidents was much higher.

HE SAID, SHE SAID

It is relatively rare for a sexual assault case to result in a trial. According to RAINN, of every 1,000 rapes, 230 are reported to police. Of those 230, only forty-six will lead to an arrest, and only five will result in a conviction. There is an old belief, stemming back to the days when women could not speak in court, that rape and sexual violence cases are especially difficult to prove. Matthew Hale was the famous seventeenth-century judge who defended the law of coverture. He also called rape "an accusation easily to be made and hard to be proved and harder to be defended by the party accused, tho never so innocent."[35] Today, this logic is commonly referred to as

SEXUAL VIOLENCE AGAINST MEN

In 2017, actor Terry Crews spoke publicly about a sexual assault that had occurred the previous year. In 2016, Crews was assaulted by a Hollywood talent agent named Adam Venit. Crews was at a party when Venit made lewd gestures at him and grabbed his genitals. In 2018, Crews testified to the US Senate about the assault. "The assault lasted only minutes, but what he was effectively telling me while he held my genitals in his hand was that he held the power," Crews said to the Senate.[1]

Crews has used his celebrity status to fight against misconceptions about sexual violence. In many ways, he does not fit the stereotypical profile of a sexual assault victim. He is a straight, black man. Crews used to be a professional football player and is tall with an athletic build. Through his testimony, Crews helped show that he experienced the same violation and sense of powerlessness as female victims of sexual violence. In addition, Crews has spoken about the difficulty victims face in finding support and justice. In a tweet, he expressed his frustration with others' questions and doubts. Crews wrote, "Why didn't you say something? I did. Why didn't you push him off? I did. Why didn't you cuss him out? I did. Why didn't you tell the police? I did. Why didn't you press charges? I did. Why did you just let it happen? I didn't. Why didn't you beat him up? (Sigh)."[2]

1. Quoted in Mahita Gajanan, "'This Happened to Me Too.' Terry Crews Details His Alleged Sexual Assault During Emotional Senate Testimony," Time, June 26, 2018. www.time.com.
2. Terry Crews, Twitter, 5:42 a.m. June 29, 2018. www.twitter.com/terrycrews.

"he said, she said." By this logic, the statements of the accused and the accuser are the only evidence involved in a sexual violence case. Since accused and accuser will give different evidence about whether an act was consensual, or whether it occurred at all, there is no way ever to know the truth.

However, in reality, there often is more evidence available aside from two people's opposing stories. "The things that I find frustrating

47

about the he-said she-said thing is that most of the time, it's really a statement that covers an inadequate investigation," says sexual violence researcher David Lisak.[36] In many cases, there is plenty of evidence that can be used to support or disprove a claim of sexual violence. Within seventy-two hours of an attack, hospitals can collect DNA evidence from attacks with what are known as rape kits, and police can collect DNA from their investigations as well. Investigators can carefully collect the testimony of the accuser and accused and see if it is truthful and supported by evidence or witnesses. They can interview people who may have witnessed some or all of an assault. Sexual violence has psychological and behavioral effects on its victims, so investigators can find out whether a victim is acting in a way that is consistent with someone who is experiencing trauma. Sexual predators often attack more than once, so investigators can find out whether an accused perpetrator has a history of sexual violence. There are resources available to thoroughly investigate and pursue sexual violence claims, but they are underused.

Even in cases in which sexual assaulters are found guilty for sexual violence, victims can suffer backlash for speaking out. In 2015, Brock Turner, a student at Stanford University, sexually assaulted an unconscious woman. He was convicted and faced a potential fourteen-year prison sentence. However, a judge only gave Turner a six-month sentence because he was worried about the "severe impact" a longer sentence would have.[37] Turner's father publicly came to his defense, saying his son had already paid "a steep price" for the assault.[38] "He will never be his happy-go-lucky self," Turner's father said.[39] A group of Turner's friends submitted sixty-one pages of letters to the judge, advocating for Turner. In response to this backlash, Turner's victim released a public statement. She recounted the damage that the assault and legal process had done to her life and her mental health. "I had to fight for an entire year to make it clear that there was something wrong with this situation," she recalled.[40]

> **"I had to fight for an entire year to make it clear that there was something wrong with this situation."**[40]
>
> —*a victim of sexual assault*

SEXUAL VIOLENCE RESPONSE IN SCHOOLS

Title IX is a law that prohibits sexual discrimination in schools and colleges. The law also contains guidelines and procedures for dealing with sexual violence and harassment. There are benefits and drawbacks to using Title IX as a way to deal with sexual violence cases. One benefit of Title IX is its lower evidentiary standard. In a jury trial, the prosecution must make a case that the accused's guilt is "beyond a reasonable doubt."[41] When students file Title IX complaints, they have a different standard, called "preponderance of evidence."[42] This means that the complainant only has to make the case that it is more likely than not that sexual violence occurred. This lower standard means that, in theory, it is easier to pursue a successful Title IX claim than to prosecute a sex crime.

However, schools and universities have a limited ability to punish Title IX violators. They can expel people who commit sexual violence and ban them from school property, but they are not obligated to report these violators to the police or to make their actions public. If a victim of sexual violence chooses to report the incident to police on her own, schools are required to cooperate with any police

Sexual violence and harassment is a problem at many schools and colleges. By law, schools and colleges must address reports of sexual harassment, but they are not required to report these incidents to police.

investigation that may occur. Additionally, under a law called the Clery Act, colleges and universities are required to keep track of and publicly release statistics on sexual assault. However, K–12 schools do not have the same obligation.

SEXUAL VIOLENCE RESPONSE IN THE MILITARY AND WORKPLACES

Sometimes, an increase in reports of sexual violence can be a sign of progress. It is a sign that people feel safe and empowered to speak out about experiences of sexual violence. In the 2017 fiscal year, the number of military sexual assault reports increased. But military representatives believe that more reporting is a sign of progress. In 2006, only one in fourteen military victims of sexual violence reported the attack. As of 2017, the military believes that number is closer to one in three. "We're seeing a bigger slice of the problem," said Nathan Galbreath, who works in the US Department of Defense's Sexual Assault Prevention and Response Office.[43] But questions remain about when and how military commanders choose to address sexual violence claims. The US military has its own legal system. In this system, the commanders in charge of investigating claims have the option to pursue cases publicly or privately. Research shows that more than 90 percent of the time, the military chooses to handle sexual assault reports privately. This means that it is difficult for those outside the chain of command to get information about sexual violence cases or understand the decision-making process behind judgments.

Since the 1970s, national conversations about sexual harassment in private organizations and companies have led to a great deal of change. According to the *Harvard Business Review*, more than 98 percent of American organizations have their own sexual harassment policies. However, research suggests that in practice, many people are punished for reporting workplace sexual harassment. One study found that three out of four employees who protested harassment faced retaliation, including punishment and negative feedback. In a 2016 report, the US government found that workplace sexual harassment training on its own was not effective in stopping harassment. Instead, the report concluded that a respectful workplace culture and clear rules about and consequences for sexual misbehavior were the best ways to counter harassment.

SEXUAL VIOLENCE IN ENTERTAINMENT

Sexual violence is commonly portrayed or discussed in TV shows, books, music, and movies. These works of entertainment reflect

When Christine Blasey Ford accused Brett Kavanaugh of sexual assault in 2018, it was not the first time a US Supreme Court nominee had faced public accusations of sexual violence. In 1991, Anita Hill testified at the confirmation hearings of Clarence Thomas, accusing him of sexual harassment. Thomas had previously been Hill's boss at the federal Equal Employment Opportunity Commission. Hill described repeated sexual harassment by Thomas while she worked with him. Despite Hill's accusations, Thomas, like Kavanaugh, was confirmed to the Supreme Court. Both Hill and Ford faced death threats after coming forward.

Several other government and political figures have also been accused of sexual violence. Former President Bill Clinton has been accused by four different women. Clinton has never been criminally charged in connection with these allegations. He has paid money to settle a sexual harassment lawsuit from one of the victims.

At least twenty-two women have accused President Donald Trump of sexual violence. He has been accused of groping, forced kissing, and rape. Trump has denied all of these allegations, saying that his accusers are lying. In 2016, however, off-air video footage from the show Access Hollywood was released showing Trump bragging in 2005 about touching and groping women against their will. Trump has said he did not mean those comments literally, calling them "locker-room talk." Trump has not been criminally charged in relation to any of these allegations.

Quoted in Meghan Keneally, "What Trump Previously Said about the 2005 'Access Hollywood' Tape That He's Now Questioning," ABC News, November 27, 2017. www.abcnews.com.

common cultural ideas about sexual violence. In some cases, popular entertainment condemns sexual violence or educates the public. Other forms of entertainment do not take sexual violence seriously or do not explore its consequences. Many pieces of entertainment media do both. In this way, popular entertainment tends to promote society's contrasting ideas about sexual violence. For instance, a 2014 study of popular teen TV dramas found that most shows in the genre portrayed rape as an evil and terrifying act. However, the study also found that rape was used casually as a plot device, mentioned or portrayed to make the show seem exciting or gritty. In these shows, acts of rape are condemned, but rapists often do not suffer consequences for their actions, and the effects of the rape on the victim character are not explored in depth. A 2017 study of unpublished movie scripts found a similar pattern. One anonymous script reader said, "[Sexual violence is] typically used as a stakes-raiser in a script that is largely about something else. It's rare that I see a script that is explicitly about sexual violence and its effects."[44]

In some cases, critics are beginning to reexamine the ways that entertainment media has portrayed sexual violence. The 1984 film *Sixteen Candles* is considered a classic teen romantic comedy. However, the movie portrays the sexual assault of an unconscious teen girl. The male romantic lead, Jake Ryan, is portrayed as an ideal teen boy. In one scene, he finds his girlfriend, a popular high school girl, unconscious on a bed after drinking heavily. Jake brags to a friend that he could rape his girlfriend at that moment and suffer no consequences but that he is too bored to do so. Instead, he shows his girlfriend to a younger boy who, the film implies, rapes her instead. The incident is portrayed as funny and lighthearted. In an essay about her early career, the film's star, Molly Ringwald, reflected on how her views on *Sixteen Candles* and other movies have changed. "If [sexist attitudes] are systemic . . . it stands to reason that the art we consume . . . plays some part in reinforcing those same attitudes," Ringwald wrote.[45]

Actress Molly Ringwald has spoken out against sexual violence in entertainment media. She has even pointed to a film she starred in, Sixteen Candles, *as an example of media not addressing sexual violence as a serious issue.*

WHO GETS TO BE A VICTIM?

Laws requiring rape victims to be virgins are in the past. But the idea that so-called "impurity" is an excuse for or invitation to rape has continued. In November 2017, a twenty-seven-year-old Irish man stood on trial for the alleged rape of a seventeen-year-old girl. The man's defense lawyer used the fact that the girl had been wearing thong underwear to argue that his client was innocent of rape. "You have to look at the way she was dressed. She was wearing a thong with a lace front," the lawyer argued in court.[46] The lawyer was drawing on ancient expectations of purity for rape victims. The defense lawyer won his case, and the twenty-seven-year-old was found not guilty of rape. The case caused an outcry in Ireland. Women posted photos of their underwear with the hashtag #ThisIsNotConsent to protest the idea that a victim's clothing could ever be considered sexual consent.

Activists have long been aware of how purity stereotypes can discredit victims. In response, in the 1970s, US states began passing what are known as "rape shield laws." These laws shield many details of an accuser's sexual history in a sexual assault trial. For example, if a female college student accuses a student she knows of sexual assault, the accused might be aware of details about the victim's sex life, like how many previous sexual partners she has had. But his lawyer would not be able to mention these details in the trial. They are not relevant to the charge of sexual assault, and they can lead judges and juries to negatively stereotype victims. Today, almost all US states have rape shield laws.

Sexual violence is common in all parts of society. It can be very difficult for victims get people to believe them, and holding attackers responsible can be even tougher. There are widespread legal and social barriers to recognizing and fighting sexual violence. In the 1970s, feminists coined a term for a society that normalizes and accepts sexual violence: *rape culture*. These critics argue that sexual violence is so accepted and so common that it warps the way people think about sex, gender, and violence. According to the feminist writer Kate Harding, "The problem . . . is the cumulative effect of so many people, working through so many [organizations] and institutions, to deliver a constant stream of [sexism] that trivializes the crime of rape and automatically awards the benefit of the doubt to the accused."[47]

HOW CAN SOCIETY PREVENT SEXUAL VIOLENCE
IN THE FUTURE?

Sexual violence is a complex societal problem. Addressing sexual violence is a legal issue, a public health issue, and a moral and cultural issue. As a result, confronting sexual violence requires multiple strategies and approaches. Some activists focus on speaking openly about experiences of sexual violence. They hope to hold attackers accountable for their actions and help victims find solidarity and support. These activists want to work toward a culture where powerful people cannot use their power for sexual abuse. Other people are focusing on reforming or reimagining the way the law handles sexual violence. Calls for police and legal reform exist alongside new legal ideas such as restorative justice. Still others are working to change rape culture into a culture where consent is understood and respected from an early age. And throughout these pushes for transformation and reform, organizations work to support victims of sexual violence and help them find justice and healing.

#METOO

In the late 1990s, activist Tarana Burke found herself talking to a thirteen-year-old girl in crisis. The girl confided to Burke that she had been sexually abused. Burke found herself not knowing how

Tarana Burke, founder of the Me Too campaign, speaks at an event in 2019. Burke started Me Too to build support for victims of sexual abuse.

to respond. "I didn't have a response or a way to help her in that moment, and I couldn't even say 'me too,'" Burke remembers.[48] The conversation later inspired her to create the nonprofit organization Just Be Inc. to help women and girls share their experiences with sexual violence. In 2006, she began a campaign to extend the reach of her work. She called the campaign Me Too.

In October 2017, the *New York Times* published an investigation into the behavior of Harvey Weinstein, a powerful and wealthy Hollywood producer. Movie producers help provide funding for films. They choose which projects receive money and resources from their studio. As a result, producers often have a great deal of influence over the moviemaking process. They can help make decisions such as which actors to hire and how much money to spend on movie publicity campaigns. The *Times* report revealed that Weinstein had used his position to sexually assault and harass actresses and employees. Weinstein admitted to some wrongdoing but denied many of the allegations against him. On October 15, 2017, actress Alyssa Milano wrote a tweet in response to the news: "Suggested by a friend: 'If all the women who have been sexually harassed or assaulted wrote 'Me too.' as a status, we might give people a sense of the magnitude of the problem.'"[49] Following the overwhelming response to Milano's tweet, #MeToo quickly became a popular social media hashtag. As of October 2018, it had been used in more than 19 million tweets. With it began the second phase of what's been called the #MeToo movement.

Many high-profile celebrities, such as model Cara Delevingne and actresses Salma Hayek and Lupita Nyong'o, added their names to the eventual list of more than eighty women accusing Weinstein of sexual misconduct. The next several months saw an explosion of discussions about the extent of sexual violence in the entertainment and media industries. The #MeToo movement spread over social media, into the political sphere, and to sectors such as the restaurant industry and academia. An October 2018 investigation by the *New York Times* found that 201 men in positions of power had lost their jobs as a result of sexual conduct publicized by #MeToo. The movement has helped empower people to come forward with stories of sexual violence and break the silence that protects offenders.

The #MeToo movement has opened public discussion of a wide variety of sexually violent behaviors, from rape to verbal sexual coercion to workplace sexual harassment. But there are people who believe that #MeToo has "gone too far."[50] Journalist Masha Gessen wrote in the *New Yorker* that she believed some #MeToo stories "blur the boundaries between rape, nonviolent sexual coercion, and bad [sex]."[51] Others have argued that the opportunity to discuss the connections between different types of sexual violence is a strength of the movement. At the news and commentary website *Slate*, journalist Christina Cauterucci argued that "If the magnitude of the movement has demonstrated anything, it's that there's an entire spectrum of sex-based abuse of power that lets those bad actors flourish."[52]

> **"If the magnitude of the [#MeToo] movement has demonstrated anything, it's that there's an entire spectrum of sex-based abuse of power that lets those bad actors flourish."** [52]
>
> – *writer Christina Cauterucci*

Although #MeToo has successfully held many people accountable for sexual violence, few of the offenders who have been publicly accused have faced legal consequences for their behavior. In May 2018, Weinstein was arrested on three sexual violence charges: first-degree rape, third-degree rape, and first-degree criminal sex act. As of October 2018, some experts believed that Weinstein's case would not go to trial. As of November 1, 2018, Weinstein also faced a lawsuit from accusers.

The #MeToo movement sparked widespread public discussions and change. But its future will depend on its ability to hold the interest of large groups of people. Some activists hope that #MeToo can help reform sexual assault laws. Historian Phyllis Thompson, who studies the history of gender and sexuality, believes #MeToo can continue to be a powerful force for change. However, she says the movement must continue to work on representing multiple perspectives. A movement like #MeToo should be one that "insists on anti-racist politics, and that doesn't tolerate structural sexism," Thompson says.[53]

The #MeToo movement has prompted discussions about sexual harassment across the world. Thousands of people have rallied in support of the movement or shared their stories on social media using the hashtag #MeToo.

But there are others who feel that the response to #MeToo should be less change. An October 2018 poll found that more than 40 percent of Americans felt that #MeToo had gone too far. Some people who were publicly accused of sexual violence during the #MeToo movement are returning to their former public lives. For example, the famous standup comedian Louis C.K. was accused of sexually harassing several women. In November 2017, he released a public statement admitting that the allegations were true. That same month, the New York premiere and distribution of his film *I Love You, Daddy* was cancelled. C.K. was fired by his management team, and several of his work projects were halted. But by August 2018 C.K. had begun performing standup again. His return to his comedy career has been met with audience approval as well as widespread criticism.

LEGAL AND POLICE REFORM

There are many ways the US criminal justice system could be improved to better serve victims of sexual violence. Some police departments are rethinking the way they interview and listen to these victims. Activists are working to release unused evidence that could help solve sexual violence cases. And prison reformers are working to shed light on the widespread problem of sexual violence within the US prison system.

The trauma of sexual violence and its effects on memory are well-known to researchers. However, people who interview sexual violence victims, including police officers and journalists, may not be aware of the way trauma affects how victims remember and discuss their own experiences. Victims may experience flashbacks and emotional distress when discussing their assaults. They also may have uneven memories of the event. In 2013, a police department in Utah developed what it called a Trauma Informed Victim Interview (TIVI) protocol. The protocol teaches officers to be aware of the ways violence affects memories and encourages them to listen to victims' stories in full. One police officer described his reaction when he learned about the biology of traumatic experiences. "Fireworks went off in my head," he remembers, "and the gaps in my cases suddenly started to fill in."[54] As a result of its experiment with TIVI, the West Valley City Police Department reported "drastic increases in the number of sexual assault cases prosecuted."[55]

Victims of sexual violence have the option to go to a hospital emergency room and tell the staff about the assault. Hospitals are required by law to offer physical exams to sexual assault victims. Victims do not have to report the crime and can decline the exam. The exam includes an account of the victim's medical history and tests for physical evidence such as hair. The victim is also examined for internal and external injuries, which are documented with photographs and samples. All of this evidence is collected and stored in what's usually called a rape kit. These kits can provide powerful evidence in investigations of sexual violence. However, experts estimate that hundreds of thousands of these rape kits have never been tested. In some cases, police departments collect the kits but do not send them away for DNA evidence. In others, the kits are sent away for testing that is not completed. Advocacy projects such as End the Backlog, which is run by the nonprofit Joyful Heart Foundation, ask for mandatory testing of these kits. The project has succeeded in raising funds to test unexamined rape kits.

SEXUAL VIOLENCE IN PRISONS

The United States has the world's largest population of incarcerated people. More than 2 million people are held in jails, prisons, juvenile correctional facilities, immigrant detention facilities, and other types of confinement. Prison inmates have very little power in their daily lives. People in prison are especially vulnerable to sexual violence by other inmates and by prison staff. The Bureau of Justice Statistics believes that more than 200,000 prison inmates a year are victims of sexual violence. People who are held in Immigration and Customs Enforcement (ICE) detention facilities are also targeted for sexual violence and abuse. In 2018, the *Intercept*, a news website, collected hundreds of accounts of sexual violence in these facilities. Many of these accounts involved sexual assault by guards and threats to force detainees into sex. Advocates believe that, because many people held in immigrant detention are afraid to report their abuse, the actual number of sexual violence incidents is much higher.

Statewide reform enacted
Statewide reform proposed
Statewide audit completed
No statewide reform

Thousands of rape kits in crime labs across the country have gone untested in what is known as the rape kit backlog. Most states have conducted statewide audits to assess how many rape kits have gone untested. As of January 2019, most of those states had also enacted reforms, such as providing more funding for rape kit testing or passing new laws to better regulate rape kit testing, according to End the Backlog, an advocacy project. Still, some state governments have not addressed the problem.

"Where the Backlog Exists and What's Happening to End It," End the Backlog, *n.d., www.endthebacklog.org.*

The Nobel Peace Prize is awarded each year to people who help advance peace in the world. The 2018 honorees, Dr. Denis Mukwege and Nadia Murad, were both recognized for their work against sexual violence.

Mukwege is a doctor from the Democratic Republic of the Congo who works with female victims of sexual violence. There have been many armed conflicts within the Democratic Republic of the Congo, and rape is used as a weapon of war in these conflicts. Mukwege founded a hospital, Panzi Hospital and Foundation, which has helped more than 50,000 victims of sexual violence. Mukwege helps heal the physical traumas of wartime rape, which can be severe. His approach also aims to treat the mental, emotional, and practical needs of victims. "We have to see the person as an entire whole," Mukwege says.[1]

Murad is a member of the Yazidi religious minority in Iraq. In 2014, Murad was kidnapped by the terrorist group ISIS. Members of the group raped her repeatedly as she was held captive. In 2015, Murad managed to escape. Today, she travels the world, telling her story and supporting other victims of sexual violence. She advocates for the other 6,000 Yazidi women who are victims of ISIS. "We have the right to speak about this," Murad says. "We have the right to deliver our message."[2]

1. Quoted in "Who Is Dr. Denis Mukwege?," Mukwege Foundation, n.d., www.mukwegefoundation.org.
2. Quoted in Morning Edition, "Nobel Winner Nadia Murad Puts a Voice to Yazidi Minority's Message," National Public Radio, October 17, 2018. www.npr.org.

In 2003, US Congress passed the Prison Rape Elimination Act. The act funded research of rape in US prisons, funded state initiatives to combat prison rape, and created new standards for dealing with prison sexual violence. Still, it was not until 2012 that the government developed standards to help inmates report sexual violence and require prison staff to respond to those reports. Between 2011 and

2015, the rate of sexual violence reports in prisons has risen by 180 percent. However, the *Marshall Project*, a criminal justice news organization, reports that "corrections administrators rarely decide that the alleged attacks actually happened. The number of accusations found to be true increased only slightly, while the number of allegations that were eventually found to be false or inconclusive skyrocketed."[56] This indicates that although more inmates are reporting sexual assault, many are still not seeing justice served in their cases.

Just Detention International (JDI) is the only nonprofit solely dedicated to fighting sexual abuse of prisoners worldwide. According to its website, JDI works to: "hold government officials accountable for prisoner rape; promote public attitudes that value the dignity and safety of people in detention; and ensure that survivors of this violence get the help they need."[57] As part of its work, JDI collects the stories of prison sexual violence victims. Clarence, who does not publicly share his last name, is an inmate in the Texas prison system. He has experienced several types of sexual violence during his time in prison. Despite his right to make complaints, Clarence reports that prison staff have retaliated against him for speaking out. He has been put in solitary confinement and denied access to prison resources such as the library. "You would not believe how common these things are," Clarence writes.[58] He believes that more action is required to help victims get justice for prison assaults.

RESTORATIVE JUSTICE

Some organizations and individuals are pursuing the option of restorative justice to better serve the needs of sexual violence victims and perpetrators. According to the Centre for Justice & Reconciliation, the process of restorative justice focuses on repairing the harm of crime, not on punishing offenders. During the restorative justice process, everyone involved in a crime meets together to discuss what happened and find a way to move forward.

Jo Nodding was raped in 2004 by a boy she knew. He was convicted and sent to prison. In 2009, both Nodding and her rapist decided they would participate in a meeting organized by a restorative justice organization. "This was about me taking control of the situation, re-balancing what he had taken away from me that day," Nodding recalls.[59] She also wanted her rapist to understand the effects of what he had done. After extensive preparation, Nodding and her attacker met. Nodding explained to her rapist how she had felt during the attack, and how it had affected her life. The perpetrator offered her an apology that she believed was sincere. In return, Nodding offered him her forgiveness. Nodding was happy that she went through the restorative justice process. "Meeting him gave me closure," she remembers, "and I had taken some kind of control over my life."[60]

Critics of restorative justice argue that the process increases the pressure that victims feel to excuse the harm that sexual violence does. They also say that in some cases restorative justice may not be an effective way to hold perpetrators accountable and remove their threat to the community. Nodding agrees that restorative justice is not appropriate for every case. "If they don't accept [wrongdoing]," Nodding says, "then restorative justice is not right for them."[61]

SEXUAL VIOLENCE EDUCATION

Many schools do not teach young students about consent at all. Only twenty-four US states require sex education for K–12 students. Of those twenty-four states, only eight have programs that teach students about sexual consent. Proponents of increased sex

ACTIVISM IN INDIA

In 2018, India was ranked the number-one most dangerous country for women. According to the Indian National Crime Records Bureau, a rape occurs about every fourteen minutes in the country. Between 2004 and 2012, about 20 million women left the Indian workforce. Experts believe that many women stay home in order to avoid sexual harassment or to protect their children from sexual violence. In 2018, cases of sexual violence against girls caused widespread outrage.

In response, Indian activists are working to combat sexual violence, harassment, and disempowerment of women. One organization, Blank Noise, uses multiple antiviolence strategies. Blank Noise focuses on helping women fight street sexual harassment and other forms of sexual violence. Blank Noise works to educate people who work on the streets, such as bus drivers, on how to see and prevent street sexual harassment. The organization's social media hashtag campaign, #INeverAskForIt, aims to fight against beliefs that blame victims for assaults. The organization also hosts listening circles, where victims and allies can meet to share their experiences. In addition, its Campus Uprising project keeps track of university projects that work against rape culture. Jasmeen Patheja, the founder of Blank Noise, described the philosophy behind her work: "We awaken the power . . . within us to become part of a movement towards creating a safe environment."

Jasmeen Patheja, "Everyone Deserves to Be Safe," TED Talks India, December 2017. www.ted.com.

education believe that younger kids deserve to start learning about sexual consent and sexual violence so they can know how to protect themselves and respect others. Some companies and nonprofits are looking for ways to strengthen consent education. Teachconsent.org, which was started by the Virginia Sexual and Domestic Violence Action Alliance, offers written and video resources for parents to talk to kids about consent. It also gives guidance to educators looking to offer consent workshops for young people. The production company Blue Seat Studios has made several videos that introduce the concept of consent to students. One of the videos has been viewed online more than 4 million times.

RESOURCES FOR SURVIVORS OF SEXUAL VIOLENCE

Activists, educators, health professionals, and sexual assault survivors are working toward a world that does not tolerate sexual violence. There is help available for victims of sexual assault. RAINN, founded in 1994, is the largest anti–sexual violence organization in the world. RAINN maintains a free hotline, 800-656-HOPE, that victims of sexual violence can call. It also offers a live chat on its website, hotline.rainn.org. The organization maintains centers where victims and their loved ones can go for counseling, medical care, and help navigating the legal system. Emergency room workers are usually trained to help victims of sexual violence, and the organization Planned Parenthood can also offer care after an attack. Many cities and regions also have local organizations that help victims of sexual violence. The National Sexual Violence Resource Center (NSVRC) maintains a directory of these local organizations. RAINN also lists local resources by state.

It can be difficult for people to see a friend or loved one deal with the aftermath of sexual violence. RAINN offers advice about supporting and listening to a survivor of sexual violence. The organization emphasizes the importance of believing victims and helping them understand that the attack was not their fault. RAINN also reminds listeners that they can help by offering nonjudgmental support. However, no one can be responsible for a friend or relative's

People can support their friends and family members who have suffered from sexual violence by listening and remaining nonjudgmental. People can also assist their loved ones in seeking professional help when dealing with sexual violence.

healing. The organization recommends telling survivors about resources such as crisis hotlines and counseling.

Experiencing sexual violence can feel lonely and overwhelming. But there is help available, and there are ways to move forward. Julianna Araujo is a survivor of child sexual abuse. She found help as an adult, and her attacker faced justice. Today, she works with RAINN to share her story online and in person. "Every time I share my story, someone comes up to me and says they have been through the same thing, have a similar story, or [I've] given them strength to take a stand," Julianna says.[62] She still copes with the wounds of sexual violence, but "every day is a healing process."[63]

SOURCE NOTES

INTRODUCTION: THE LARRY NASSAR HEARING

1. Quoted in CNN, "Watch Aly Raisman Confront Larry Nassar in Court," *YouTube*, January 19, 2018. www.youtube.com.

2. Quoted in CNN, "Watch Aly Raisman Confront Larry Nassar in Court."

3. Quoted in Eric Levenson, "This Gymnast is Now the First Man to Accuse Larry Nassar of Abuse," *CNN*, March 6, 2018. www.cnn.com.

4. Quoted in Will Hobson, "Twenty Years of Failure: Many Groups Missed Chances to Stop Larry Nassar," *Washington Post*, January 26, 2018. www.washingtonpost.com.

5. Quoted in Hobson, "Twenty Years of Failure: Many Groups Missed Chances to Stop Larry Nassar."

6. Quoted in Will Hobson, "Larry Nassar, Former USA Gymnastics Doctor, Sentenced to 40–175 Years for Sex Crimes," *Washington Post*, January 24, 2018. www.washingtonpost.com.

7. Quoted in Dan Barry, Serge F. Kovaleski, and Juliet Macur, "As F.B.I. Took a Year to Pursue the Nassar Case, Dozens Say They Were Molested," *Washington Post*, February 3, 2018. www.washingtonpost.com.

8. "Sexual Assault," *Rape, Abuse, and Incest National Network*, n.d. www.rainn.org.

CHAPTER 1: WHAT IS THE HISTORY BEHIND SEXUAL VIOLENCE?

9. Mark Peters, "The History of the Word Rape," *Good*, February 3, 2011. www.good.is.

10. "Deuteronomy 22," *Bible Gateway*, n.d. www.biblegateway.com.

11. Susan Brownmiller, *Against Our Will: Men, Women and Rape*. New York: Simon and Schuster, 1975. p. 26.

12. Quoted in Eric Berkowitz, "'The Rape-Your-Wife Privilege': The Horrifying Modern History of Marital Rape," *Salon*, August 8, 2015. www.salon.com.

13. Bernice Yeung, *In a Day's Work: The Hidden Story of Sexual Violence against America's Most Vulnerable Workers*. New York: The New Press, 2018. p. 104.

14. Quoted in "On Slaveholders' Sexual Abuse of Slaves," *National Humanities Center*, n.d. www.nationalhumanitiescenter.org.

15. Quoted in Michel Martin, "Recy Taylor's Rape Still Haunts Us," *National Public Radio*, January 14, 2018. www.npr.org.

16. Quoted in Rachel Cooke, "US Feminist Susan Brownmiller on Why Her Groundbreaking Book on Rape Is Still Relevant," *Guardian*, February 18, 2018. www.theguardian.com.

17. Quoted in Sascha Cohen, "How a Book Changed the Way We Talk about Rape," *Time*, October 9, 2015. www.time.com.

18. Quoted in David Margolick, "Marital Rape: Law's Critics Join an Appeal," *New York Times*, December 18, 1984. www.nytimes.com.

CHAPTER 2: HOW DOES SEXUAL VIOLENCE HAPPEN?

19. David Lisak and Paul Miller, "Repeat Rape and Multiple Offending Among Undetected Rapists," *Violence and Victims*, 2002. www.davidlisak.com.

20. Jon Krakauer, *Missoula: Rape and the Justice System in a College Town*. New York: Doubleday, 2015. p. 102.

21. Roxane Gay, *Hunger: A Memoir of (My) Body*. New York: Harper, 2017. p. 9.

22. Gay, *Hunger: A Memoir of (My) Body*.

23. Quoted in Mara Gordon, "Sexual Assault and Harassment May Have Lasting Health Repercussions for Women," *National Public Radio*, October 3, 2018. www.npr.com.

24. Quoted in Alex Shephard, "Minutes, News & Notes: Christine Blasey Ford," *New Republic*, November 2018. www.newrepublic.com.

25. *The Hunting Ground*. Directed by Kirby Dick and Amy Ziering, Chain Camera Pictures, 2015.

26. Quoted in Daniella Silva, "McDonald's Workers Go on Strike over Sexual Harassment," *NBC News*, September 18, 2018. www.nbcnews.com.

27. Quoted in Kari Lydersen, "'I'm Not on the Menu': McDonald's Workers Strike over 'Rampant' Sexual Harassment," *Guardian*, September 18, 2018. www.theguardian.com.

28. Quoted in Zachary Cohen, "From Fellow Soldier to 'Monster' in Uniform: #MeToo in the Military," *CNN*, February 7, 2018. www.cnn.com.

29. Quoted in *Breaking Silence*. Directed by Nadya Ali, 2017.

30. Quoted in *Breaking Silence*.

31. "40th Statewide Investigating Grand Jury Report 1 Interim – Redacted," *The Unified Judicial System of Pennsylvania*, 2018. www.pacourts.us.

32. Quoted in Alia E. Dastagir, "She Was Sexually Assaulted Within Months of Coming Out. She's Not Alone," *USA Today*, June 13, 2018. www.usatoday.com.

CHAPTER 3: HOW DOES SOCIETY RESPOND TO SEXUAL VIOLENCE?

33. Cory R. Yung, "How to Lie with Rape Statistics: America's Hidden Rape Crisis." *Iowa Law Review*, vol. 99, no. 3, 2014. pp. 1197–1256.

34. Krakauer, *Missoula: Rape and the Justice System in a College Town*. p. 54.

35. Quoted in Julie Bindel, "Rape: A Burning Injustice," *Guardian*, August 13, 2013. www.theguardian.com.

36. Quoted in Bernice Yeung, *In a Day's Work: The Hidden Story of Sexual Violence against America's Most Vulnerable Workers*. New York: The New Press, 2018. p. 105.

37. Quoted in Katie J.M. Baker, "Here's the Powerful Letter the Stanford Victim Read to Her Attacker," *Buzzfeed News*, June 3, 2019. www.buzzfeednews.com.

38. Quoted in Elle Hunt, "'20 Minutes of Action': Father Defends Stanford Student Son Convicted of Sexual Assault," *Guardian*, June 5, 2016. www.theguardian.com.

39. Quoted in Hunt, "'20 Minutes of Action': Father Defends Stanford Student Son Convicted of Sexual Assault."

40. Quoted in Baker, "Here's the Powerful Letter the Stanford Victim Read to Her Attacker."

41. Quoted in Claire Hansen, "New Title IX Guidance Gives Schools Choice in Sexual Misconduct Cases," *US News & World Report*, September 26, 2017. www.usnews.com.

42. Quoted in "Title IX," *End Rape on Campus*, n.d. www.endrapeoncampus.org.

43. Quoted in Lisa Ferdinando, "DoD Releases Annual Report on Sexual Assault in Military," *Health.mil*, May 3, 2018. www.health.mil.

44. Quoted in Kate Hagen, "Sexual Violence in Spec Screenplays," *The Black List*, October 16, 2017. blog.blcklst.com.

45. Molly Ringwald, "What About 'The Breakfast Club'?" *New Yorker*, April 6, 2018. www.newyorker.com.

46. Quoted in Marie O'Halloran, "TD Holds Up Thong in Dáil in Protest at Cork Rape Trial Comments," *Irish Times*, November 13, 2018. www.irishtimes.com.

47. Kate Harding, *The Alarming Rise of Rape Culture—and What We Can Do about It*. Boston, MA: Perseus Books Group, 2015. p. 6.

CHAPTER 4: HOW CAN SOCIETY PREVENT SEXUAL VIOLENCE IN THE FUTURE?

48. Quoted in Sandra E. Garcia, "The Woman Who Created #MeToo Long Before Hashtags," *New York Times*, October 20, 2017. www.nytimes.com.

49. Alyssa Milano, *Twitter*, 1:21 p.m., October 15, 2017. www.twitter.com/Alyssa_Milano.

50. Masha Gessen, *Twitter*, 4:03 p.m., December 7, 2017. www.twitter.com/mashagessen.

51. Masha Gessen, "When Does a Watershed Become a Sex Panic?" *New Yorker*, November 14, 2017. www.newyorker.com.

52. Christina Cauterucci, "For God's Sake, *New York Times*, #MeToo Is Not Going to End Flirting and Fun Sex," *Slate*, January 5, 2018. www.slate.com.

53. Quoted in Christina Pazzanese and Colleen Walsh, "The Women's Revolt: Why Now, and Where To," *Harvard Gazette*, December 21, 2017. news.harvard.edu.

54. Quoted in Justin Boardman, "How to More Effectively Interview Traumatized Sexual Violence Victims," *Campus Safety*, June 12, 2017. www.campussafetymagazine.com.

55. "Groundbreaking WVCPD Sexual Assault Protocol Drastically Increases Prosecution Rates," *West Valley City Police*, April 13, 2016. www.wvc-ut.gov.

56. Alysia Santo, "Prison Rape Allegations Are on the Rise," *Marshall Project*, July 25, 2018. www.themarshallproject.org.

57. "Our Mission," *Just Detention International*, n.d. www.justdetention.org.

58. "Survival Stories: Clarence, Texas," *Just Detention International*, n.d. www.justdetention.org.

59. Jo Nodding, "Jo Nodding," *The Forgiveness Project*, n.d. www.theforgivenessproject.com.

60. Nodding, "Jo Nodding."

61. Paul Crosland, "Jo Nodding, Restorative Justice Interview in Full, 13th September 2011," *YouTube*, September 13, 2011. www.youtube.com.

62. "Julianna's Story," *Rape, Abuse, and Incest National Network*, n.d. www.rainn.org.

63. "Julianna's Story."

FOR FURTHER RESEARCH

BOOKS

Olivia Ghafoerkhan, *Sexual Assault: The Ultimate Teen Guide*. Lanham, MD: Rowman & Littlefield, 2017.

Kate Harding, *Asking for It: The Alarming Rise of Rape Culture—and What We Can Do about It*. Boston, MA: Perseus Books Group, 2015.

Rebecca Rissman, *Rape Culture and Sexual Violence*. Minneapolis, MN: Abdo Publishing, 2018.

Bernice Yeung, *In a Day's Work: The Hidden Story of Sexual Violence against America's Most Vulnerable Workers*. New York: The New Press, 2018.

INTERNET SOURCES

Allie Conti, "A Brief and Depressing History of Rape Laws," *Vice*, June 8, 2016. www.vice.com.

Alia E. Dastagir, "She Was Sexually Assaulted within Months of Coming Out. She Isn't Alone," *USA Today*, June 13, 2018. www.usatoday.com.

Tara Golshan, "Study Finds 75 Percent of Workplace Harassment Victims Experienced Retaliation When They Spoke Up," *Vox*, October 15, 2017. www.vox.com.

Sandra Gonzalez, Lisa Respers France, and Chloe Melas, "The Year since the Weinstein Scandal First Rocked Hollywood," *CNN*, October 4, 2018. www.cnn.com.

WEBSITES

Rape, Abuse & Incest National Network (RAINN)

www.RAINN.org

RAINN is the largest nonprofit organization committed to helping victims of sexual violence.

Scarleteen

www.scarleteen.com

Scarleteen is a website that provides information on sexual health. It offers guidelines and information on consent, sexual violence, and sexual abuse.

US Centers for Disease Control and Prevention (CDC)

www.cdc.gov

Part of the CDC's work is to conduct research on sexual violence. The agency provides information about this problem, methods to help people who have suffered sexual violence, and strategies for communities to try to prevent this problem.

INDEX

INDEX CONTINUED

ABOUT THE AUTHOR

A.W. Buckey is a writer living in Brooklyn, New York.